THE MAGIC LINK

Piano Albums by Schumann and Tchaikovsky

Masterclass with Rada Bukhman

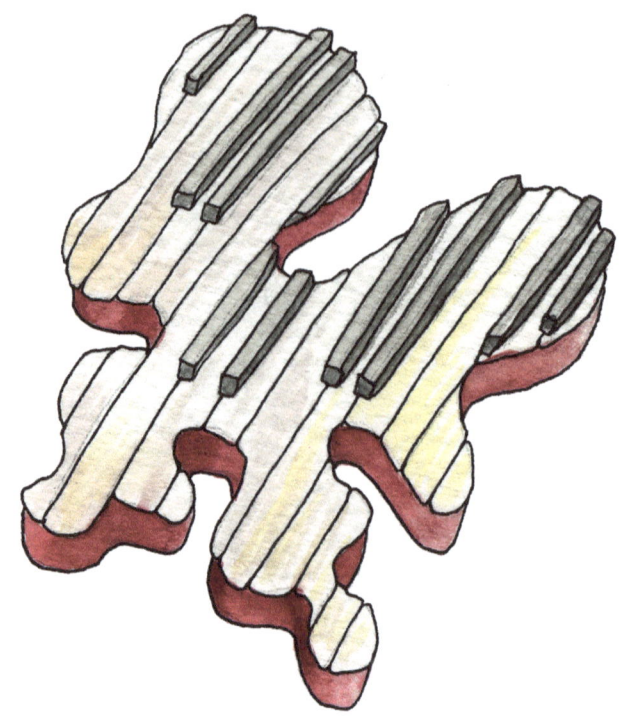

Illustrations: Rada Bukhman and her students: Elsie Lu, Esther Lee, Jingchen Ma, Sarah Yang, and Rebecca Bukhman

Book Cover: Anna Vetrova

Photography and Digital Images Processing: Alexander Bukhman

Music Notation and Layout Editing: Anna Yuferova

Text Editing: Julie Sutherland

Copyright©2013 by Rada Bukhman

Notice of Rights:
All rights reserved. Except for brief quotations in a review, this book or parts thereof must not be reproduced in any form by any means, electronic, mechanical, photocopying, recording, or otherwise, without the prior written permission of the author.
For information please contact the author through the following website: www.radabukhman.com

Notice of Liability:
While every precaution has been taken in preparation of this book, the author shall have no liability whatsoever to any person or entity with respect to any loss or damage caused or alleged to be caused directly or indirectly by any part of the content or the instructions contained in this book.

ISBN: 978-0-9918225-1-5

TABLE OF CONTENTS

Preface 5
The Story of Children's Albums 7
Keeping J.S. Bach in Mind 9
    P. Tchaikovsky, Morning Prayer 9
    R. Schumann, Chorale 10
Enchanting Marches 14
    R. Schumann, Soldier's March 14
    P. Tchaikovsky, March of the Wooden Soldiers 16
Paying Homage to Beethoven and Mendelssohn 20
    R. Schumann, Happy Farmer 20
    R. Schumann, Little Song without Words 22
    R. Schumann, Remembrance 24
Making the Piano Sing 26
    R. Schumann, Romance 26
    P. Tchaikovsky, Sweet Dream 28
Wooden Horses 32
    R. Schumann, Wild Horseman 32
    P. Tchaikovsky, Playing Hobby-Horses 34
Sad Tales 37
    P. Tchaikovsky, Sick Doll 39
    P. Tchaikovsky, Funeral March 41
    R. Schumann, First Loss 44
    R. Schumann, Mignon 47
Dancing with the Doll 49
    P. Tchaikovsky, Waltz 49
    P. Tchaikovsky, New Doll 54
    P. Tchaikovsky, Mazurka 56
    P. Tchaikovsky, Polka 59
Folk Tunes 61
    P. Tchaikovsky, Neapolitan Song 61
    P. Tchaikovsky, Old French Song 63
    P. Tchaikovsky, German Song 65
    P. Tchaikovsky, Russian Song 66
    P. Tchaikovsky, Kamarinskaya 67
    P. Tchaikovsky, Harmonica Player 70
    P. Tchaikovsky, Organ Grinder Sings 73
When the Spring Comes 74
    R. Schumann May, Sweet May 74
    R. Schumann, Folk Song 78
    P. Tchaikovsky, Song of the Lark 81

An Italian Journey 85
    P. Tchaikovsky, Italian Song...... 85
    R. Schumann, Sicilienne 87

Winter Time 91
    P. Tchaikovsky, Winter Morning 91
    R. Schumann, Winter Time 94
    P. Tchaikovsky, Mama 96

Fairytales 98
    R. Schumann, Humming Song 98
    R. Schumann, Melody 100
    P. Tchaikovsky, Nanny Tells a Story 103
    P. Tchaikovsky, Baba Yaga 107
    R. Schumann Knight Rupert 110

Chorales and Carols 114
    P. Tchaikovsky, In the Church 114
    R. Schumann, Figured Chorale 116
    R. Schumann, New Year's Eve 119

PREFACE

For more than a century, Schumann and Tchaikovsky's piano albums for children have brought enormous value to the process of developing young musicians. This music has continued to inspire famous performers into their adulthood. Pianists like Alexander Goldenweizer, Mikhail Pletnev, Idil Biret, Carlo Zecchi, and Alexis Weissenberg have all included it in their concert repertoire.

The genre of children's collections finds its roots in the second *Notebook of Anna Magdalena Bach*, who collected music of different composers for the educational needs of her children and for students of her renowned husband, J.S. Bach.

Schumann brought new features into his *Album*: program music with a narrative and learning tips for young musicians.

Inspired by Schumann's creation, Tchaikovsky composed his version of an *Album*, continuing the idea of program music that evokes pictures and impressions of a child's life.

Both *Albums* are written for children, but the musical language of these genius composers and the thematic content of the compositions are very challenging to comprehend without serious musical education. Thus, this music must be explained to young performers by an experienced teacher. The main purpose of this book is to teach how to analyze and understand the music and have the students not only develop technically but also become involved in the much greater aspects of piano playing and musicianship.

This book describes to children how the composers worked, what inspired them, how one composer influenced another, how to understand the composers' musical language, and how to find the narrative behind a musical composition.

These serious topics are discussed in the form of a lesson with a teacher and a few students, making it entertaining and easy to read - even for children.

The book includes carefully verified and edited scores of entire *Children's Album* by Tchaikovsky and part of Schumann's *Album for the Young*.

THE STORY OF CHILDREN'S ALBUMS

In a studio a teacher is sitting in front of the piano with a few of her students getting ready for an unusual lesson. They won't play scales or studies today. They will not work on any particular piano technique. They won't even practise their new repertoire. This will come another time. Today they will explore music in a different way and on a different level. The teacher places the scores of Schumann's 'Album for the Young' and Tchaikovsky's 'Children's Album' on the music stand and the masterclass begins:

Teacher: "Music is a language" – this is a mantra musicians like to repeat. But playing a musical piece, even fluently and without mistakes, is still far from speaking this language. It is like comparing a robot saying a sentence expressionlessly with an emotional song performed by a human being. There is something that each composer wants us to feel and understand when transforming his or her manuscript into music. Those black and white notes, signs of dynamics and articulation, are there to tell us a story: sometimes a scary or a sad one, sometimes a joyful and funny one. It could be full of passion, or it might be relaxed and tranquil. Composers trust that performers will communicate their music to the listeners exactly the way they want it to sound. Thus we – the performers – must learn the composers' language. (And some of them speak very different musical languages!) We need to research, understand, and implement the composers' ideas to bring them to the listeners.

"So, how exactly is the music composed?" wonders **Tom**.

"How do composers get their ideas?" asks **Mary**, joining the discussion.

"How do they get inspired?" wonders **Jenny**.

"I can compose!" exclaims little **Rebecca**, striking the piano keys with great enthusiasm.

Teacher: Why don't we take our favourite children's piano cycles by Robert Schumann and Pyotr Ilyich Tchaikovsky and try to reveal the meaning of their musical content? First of all, we need to know when and why Schumann and Tchaikovsky created those piano albums.

When German composer Robert Schumann was a child, he hesitated to choose what he liked more – music or literature. He was superior in both fields. Enjoying writing and composing, playing instruments and reading serious books, young Robert couldn't imagine that one day he would be forced by his family to go to a university to study a subject beyond his interests – law.

A few decades later, the same story happened in Russia with yet another gifted child – Pyotr Tchaikovsky. Although his parents recognized Pyotr's predisposition to music, they decided that the career of a musician was too risky. When Pyotr was 10 years old, his family enrolled him into the School of Jurisprudence to study theory of law.

However, with age and experience, both Schumann and Tchaikovsky managed to dedicate themselves fully to music, answering their life callings. They became two of the most important composers of 19th century. Both composers wrote symphonies and serious works for piano and other instruments. Music for children wasn't in the scope of their work. However one day, things changed.

Robert Schumann and his wife Clara, an amazing pianist, had many children. Robert was a very devoted and loving father. When his eldest daughter, Marie, was about to turn seven, he decided to create a musical gift for her by composing a few piano pieces so she could play them by herself. The humility of his initial plan was defeated by inspiration – instead of a few compositions, Schumann created a collection of 48 beautiful pieces that were unified by a few themes. Schumann considered his collection to be a valuable addition to children's repertoire, which was limited at that time. He even included a list of rules for young musicians, such as *Always insist on having your instrument purely tuned*, or *Always play as if a master was listening to you*. This beautiful piano cycle is well known under the name of *Album for the Young*. When Schumann's youngest daughter, Eugenia, was writing her book of memories, she included brief but impressive reminiscences of piano lessons with her extraordinary mother Clara, many of which related to the *Album for the Young*. Later, we will discuss some of those priceless recollections.

Thirty years later, Pyotr Ilyich Tchaikovsky, who admired Schumann's music, followed a similar path. While visiting his relatives in Ukraine, after a long European trip, he often listened to his little nephews practising piano. Just like Schumann, he became upset realizing how limited and primitive the children's repertoire was. As a result, the composer created a piano cycle of 24 colourful pieces, *Children's Album*, and dedicated it to his young, musically-gifted nephew, Volodja Davydov.

Each *Album* is unique; however, there are similarities in their musical language and chosen themes. Tchaikovsky credited Schumann's influence by writing on the title page: *In imitation of Schumann*.

Rebecca: Why are there no pictures in the music book?

Teacher: Unfortunately, Schumann's dream to illustrate each piece of the *Album* wasn't implemented. In its first edition, Tchaikovsky's album did have illustrations, though the composer wasn't really happy with them. "These illustrations are far from a painting of the Sistine Madonna, but they may amuse children," – commented the composer sarcastically.

Tom: Who is going to illustrate our journey?

Teacher: I have a few young artists who volunteered to help us! So let's begin our musical adventure. Turn the page…

KEEPING J. S. BACH IN MIND

Morning Prayer

P.I. Tchaikovsky

Teacher: Tchaikovsky opens his *Album* addressing his music to God. Of what does the sound of *Morning Prayer* remind you?

Jenny: It sounds as if we're listening to the choir in church.

Teacher: You are correct; it sounds like a multi-voiced choral piece performed during church ceremonies. How did the composer manage to create this effect? Look at the scores; what do you see?

Tom: Various chords?

Teacher: True, there are chords if we follow the vertical line of music. However, if we pay attention to the horizontal development of the musical material, we might discover quite a few independent melody lines – a few different voices. Each line develops individually, but all together they create beautiful harmonies. When composers write music for a choir, they use this technique.

Look at the music and tell us how many voices there are in the piece.

Tom: There are four voices: two high and two low.

Teacher: Remember their names: *Bass, Tenor, Alto,* and *Soprano*. Tchaikovsky blends those voices to create the effect of a bell ringing. At the end of the *Morning Prayer*, he uses a drone bass in one hand, while supporting sonorous descending chords in another. Bell ringing played – and still plays – a very important role in the traditions of the Russian Orthodox Church. Not only do they have the practical uses of announcing the time and calling people to prayer, but their beauty is meant to evoke spiritual feelings as well.

Now let's open Schumann's *Album for the Young* and find the piece entitled *Chorale*.

Teacher: Like many other great composers, Schumann was inspired by the music of J.S. Bach. His short piece uses the theme of Bach's *Chorale* from *Cantata 32*.
Listen to the Bach's theme:

Teacher: How did Schumann modify the theme?

Mary: He is using half notes instead of quarter notes.

Teacher: Yes, he is changing the value of the notes, but he is also changing the time signature. There is an *alla breve* sign, which means that we should consider the half note as one beat. Thus, the pulse is similar to Bach's *Chorale*. How is this music related to Tchaikovsky's *Morning Prayer*?

Jenny: Similar to *Morning Prayer*, it sounds like a choir.

Mary: Additionally, both pieces are written in G Major. The music is bright and soulful.

Teacher: Many composers of the Baroque period used the choice of the key in relation to the character of the piece. We cannot always apply this rule to Bach's music since he used to transpose a lot (rewrite his piece in the different key). However, examining his keyboard music in G Major, we do feel that this key often represents an atmosphere of calmness and joy.

Now, we are going to continue searching for connections between composers while moving to a different type of musical genre. In the very beginning of each of the *Albums*, both composers included marches, a very popular music form in their ages that was often heard in the streets. Let's define the *march*.

Tom: It is for soldiers!

Jenny: The march has four beats in each bar.

Rebecca: I like marching and playing drums - just like in parades!

Teacher: In addition to its usefulness, the march also gained the status of an independent musical genre. Marches are found in the earliest collections of keyboard music.

ENCHANTING MARCHES

Soldier's March

Lively and precise

R. Schumann

Teacher: What can you say about character of Schumann's music?

Tom: It is playful.

Rebecca: It sounds funny and happy! Jump! Jump! Jump!

Teacher: Very good! Schumann's march is also humorous. It doesn't sound like a real military march. I'll show you where the theme comes from. Please examine the *Scherzo* in Beethoven's *Sonata No. 5 for violin and piano, Op. 24, Spring.*

Tom: Did Schumann borrow ideas from the other composers quite often?

Teacher: No, he didn't exactly borrow ideas; rather, he absorbed everything he read, saw, or heard around him. Later, he unconsciously shaped it into his music. In addition, Schumann enjoyed quoting his musical idols, thereby sharing his personal admiration with others.

Jenny: When they compose, do they play the music first and write it down later?

Teacher: Good question! Some composers like J.S. Bach, Brahms, and Shostakovich didn't need an instrument. Mozart often composed on a billiard table! Other composers like Chopin, Grieg, and Prokofiev had to check the sound on the piano before writing it down. Schumann always worked with an instrument, while Tchaikovsky usually didn't need one. I know some contemporary composers who compose in the car or even in an airplane!

Now let's see what you have to say about Tchaikovsky's version of the march – his March of the Wooden Soldiers.

March of the Wooden Soldiers

P.I. Tchaikovsky

Jenny: The music is light and not loud.

Tom: The rhythm is similar to Schumann's march. I like the sound of drum in the left hand: *ti di-li ti-ti*.

Teacher: The soldiers in Tchaikovsky's march are not real; they are toy soldiers. Thus, this march is very light and even gracious. The composer indicates *piano* as a dynamic to avoid a heavy touch in performance.

Rebecca: It sounds like a *Nutcracker*!

Teacher: Actually it does remind us of the march from Tchaikovsky's famous ballet, *The Nutcracker*.

Teacher: When we talked about Schumann's march a bit earlier, we looked into Beethoven's scores. Beethoven was the last greatest composer of the Classical period. Schumann had enormous respect for Beethoven's authority. Another piece by Schumann that can be traced to Beethoven's influence is *Happy Farmer*.

PAYING HOMAGE TO BEETHOVEN AND MENDELSSOHN

Happy Farmer

R. Schumann

Teacher: Beethoven's *Pastoral Symphony No. 6* musically portrays the countryside; it reflects an idyllic atmosphere and the happiness of being. In fact, the third part of the symphony is called *Merry Gathering of Country People*. The melody of Schumann's piece sounds very similar to the main theme of this part, and the key is the same – F major.

Teacher: Clara Schumann taught her daughter Eugenia to play *Happy Farmer* in moderate tempo because it's said that peasants never hurry – neither in work, nor in their dances. She said that at the beginning of the piece, it is the father farmer who is singing alone. Later (in the middle part), his little son joins him.

Mary: Was Schumann good friends with Beethoven?

Teacher: No, Schumann never met Beethoven, who was 40 years older. He did meet and befriend other composers, however. For example, he was very close friends with Felix Mendelssohn – one of the most important composers of the Romantic era.

Jenny: Why is he important? Was his music special?

Teacher: Not only was Mendelssohn a great composer, but he also deserves to be remembered and acknowledged for the reintroduction of J.S. Bach's music to the public. It is hard to imagine, but J.S. Bach's music was almost forgotten for more than 100 years.

Tom: How did Mendelssohn bring this music back to the world?

Teacher: One day when Felix was 15 years old, his grandmother brought him a copy of the score of Bach's *St. Matthew Passion*. Mendelssohn examined the music and became ecstatic. He decided to prepare the whole work for performance. It took him five long years to arrange the score and rehearse this gigantic work, and his efforts were rewarded in the best possible way: From that point on, Bach's music was researched extensively, edited, arranged, and performed.

Jenny: What is Mendelssohn's music like?

Teacher: Mendelssohn was a master of very expressive melodies. His *Violin Concerto in E Minor* is one of the most beloved pieces, highlighted by its beautiful main theme. Mendelssohn created the new sub-genre of lyrical piano miniatures *Songs without Words*, which evokes feelings of romance. His idea was to make the piano sound like a voice, expressing emotions on the most intimate level. Each piece imitates a vocal melody with a piano accompaniment and uses a variety of piano techniques. Mendelssohn wrote a generous collection of these "songs," inspiring other contemporaries participate in this musical form.

Rebecca: Why would he write a song without words? That is weird. I like to sing songs *with* words!

Teacher: This is an instrumental genre. His songs are meant to be performed solely by a pianist. In fact, he objected to a poet friend's idea to add words to the music. He said: "What the music I love expresses to me is not thought too indefinite to put into words, but on the contrary, too definite."

Mary: Did Schumann compose "songs without words"?

Teacher: Yes he did! He included in his *Album Little Song without Words*. In fact, Schumann indicated on his score that this piece should be played after completing one's homework.

Rebecca: Why after homework?

Teacher: He was probably offering it as a treat because the piece is fairly easy to perform.

Little Song without Words

Teacher: Schumann also included another piece in his *Album* in the genre of *Songs without Words*. It was entitled *Remembrance* and was a farewell to his dearest friend Mendelssohn, who unfortunately lived a very short life.

Remembrance
(4 November 1847)

R. Schumann

MAKING THE PIANO SING

Tom: You said earlier that *Songs without Words* sound like a romance. What exactly is "romance"?

Teacher: The word "romance" is used for intimate, lyrical vocal and instrumental pieces. The roots of this musical genre can be found in French *ballades*. It was originally a genre of poetry, but Schubert created its vocal alternative, and then Chopin made this genre instrumental, composing a cycle of four *ballades* for the piano. If we listen to the piece called *Romance* from Schumann's *Album*, we can clearly hear the link to the first *ballade* by Chopin in G Minor. It bears the same declamatory style of melody, accompanied by light chords imitating an accompaniment by a string instrument - like the guitar.

Romance

R. Schumann

Teacher: Tchaikovsky was a true master of vocal music. Besides multiple operas, he wrote a large number of very beautiful romances. Romances were part of his composing activities throughout his lifetime. *Sweet Dream* from the *Album* is an example of a soulful, gentle, and beautiful instrumental version of a romance. Or, we can call it a "song without words." The melody moves from the high register to the low and back again, as if a violin and cello are taking turns. Sometimes they create a duet, while the melody in both voices moves together at the same time.

WOODEN HORSES

Teacher: Now, let's have some fun. Each *Album* has a few themes that correspond directly to a child's world. What do children like the most?

Rebecca: I like to play with dolls!

Tom: I like stories.

Jenny: I like everything!

Teacher: You will find everything in this music. We will start with toys and games. In the olden days, boys liked to ride wooden horses. In Schumann's *Album*, there is a piece that every child learning piano wants to try. Can you guess which piece is it? Who is riding a horse in Schumann's cycle?

Tom: The "wild horseman"!

Teacher: Correct! Take a look in the score. There are *sforzandos* here and there along the melody line. Schumann's daughter Eugenia mentions in her dairies that her *sforzandos* were too soft and unclear until her mother, Clara Schumann, told her that she has to imagine an energetic boy skipping around the room on a stick-horse, randomly bumping into the furniture. This image helped Eugenia to play *sforzandos* comfortably and make them sound meaningful.

Wild Horseman

Teacher: The sound of horses and spurs in Tchaikovsky's *Album* come from a little *toccata* called *Playing Hobby-Horses*. You can see that the articulation (staccato) and rhythmical pattern of triplets serves to recreate the feeling of racing horses.

Tom: The articulation and rhythm sounds similar to Schumann's *Wild Horseman*.

Teacher: The structure of phrases and the development of the melody line, however, are different, and it affects the character of the pieces. Schumann's rider starts from the upbeat, and the melody goes up by large intervals, contributing to the feeling of speed and movement. Tchaikovsky's horses are not as wild. The melody moves in steps, and the beat is steady. You can feel that the horses are under control!

SAD TALES

Rebecca: Now, let's talk about dolls!

Teacher: Tchaikovsky included a trilogy about a doll in his cycle. The story starts sadly: The doll becomes sick, which is expressed musically through the use of a minor key, a slow pulse, and an expressive melody line. Notice the intonation in the melody (G – F sharp); it sounds like a sad exhale. The interval of a minor second is often used to imitate suffering. Let's have a look at the score of another piece by Tchaikovsky; the *Autumn Song*. This is part of his *The Seasons* cycle. As in the case with the *Sick Doll*, the melody begins off-beat from the "sad exhale" and in the high register.

Teacher: The *Sick Doll* expresses the feelings of the girl who owned the doll. This is an actual situation Tchaikovsky happened to observe. Thus, the music sounds very serious, very melodramatic.

Rebecca: How can the doll get sick if she is not real? Did she forget to wash her hands?

Teacher: Dolls can get sick in many different ways. For example, when I was a little girl, my older brother decided to figure out what my favourite doll looked like inside. After his experiment, my doll was really sick; I would say her "disease" was fatal. I guess Tchaikovsky's doll suffered the same fate since the *Funeral March* in C minor follows the *Sick Doll* piece. This key, C minor, was very special for composers of the earlier classical period, especially for Beethoven, who often used it for his most dramatic compositions (for instance, *Symphony No. 5*, a few sonatas for piano, *Concerto for Piano No. 3*, *32 Variations for Piano*.) I assume it is not a coincidence that Tchaikovsky used C minor for a tragic piece. *Funeral March* was excluded from the early editions of Tchaikovsky's *Album*. I guess the publishers tried to avoid upsetting children, but later it was restored to the cycle.

Sick Doll

P.I. Tchaikovsky

Funeral March

P.I. Tchaikovsky

Adagio

Teacher: When Schumann was preparing his *Album* for publishing, he intended to have nice illustrations. He invited a German artist, Ludwig Richter, to listen to Clara perform his music. Schumann then explained the idea of each piece. As a result, the piece, *First Loss*, was accompanied by an illustration of a young girl mourning a dead bird, an unhappy event that took place in the Schumann home. The melody line of *First Loss* starts with the same notes as those in the *Sick doll*: G – F#. The opening descending half-step often serves as the musical symbol of suffering. Romantic composers inherited this symbol from J.S. Bach. In the middle part of the piece, where suffering turns to dramatic pathos, Schumann explores a variety of composing techniques: frequent harmony changes and "imitation" (repetition of a melody in a different voice). Schumann had been enthusiastically studying Bach, but his own polyphony has more freedom in structure.

Teacher: Schumann loved poetry as much as he loved music. Poetry was one of his major inspirations for composing new music. One of the pieces in the *Album* portrays a teenage girl, Mignon – the main character of a poem by the great German poet Goethe. When she was a child, Mignon got lost and couldn't find her way back home. She was abducted by a group of circus artists and became a circus artist herself, dancing on a tightrope.

Jenny: What happened to her? Did she find her parents?

Teacher: No, she never returned to her homeland. You'll read this story when you are older. Eugenia Schumann mentioned that this was the piece in the album that her mother loved most. The music resonated with Clara's personality – melancholy, pure, and soulful. Interestingly, when Clara was a little girl, she was touring Germany, giving solo recitals. After one of the performances she received a medal from Goethe himself with his portrait and the following words inscribed on it: "For the gifted artist Clara Wieck."

DANCING WITH THE DOLL

Rebecca: I don't like sad songs! Can we play something happy?

Teacher: Tchaikovsky finished his trilogy about a doll on a positive note. After the *Funeral March*, there is a twirling and exhilarating waltz, followed by the *New Doll* piece.

Rebecca: Was the new doll dancing this waltz?

Teacher: We can imagine that. The theme of *New Doll* developed from the musical material of waltz, with its short, impetuous motives. Tchaikovsky often used the genre of the waltz. He included a waltz in his *Sixth Symphony*, *The Pathétique*, in a very unusual time signature. Instead of the traditional 3/4, he states it in 5/4.

Waltz

P.I. Tchaikovsky

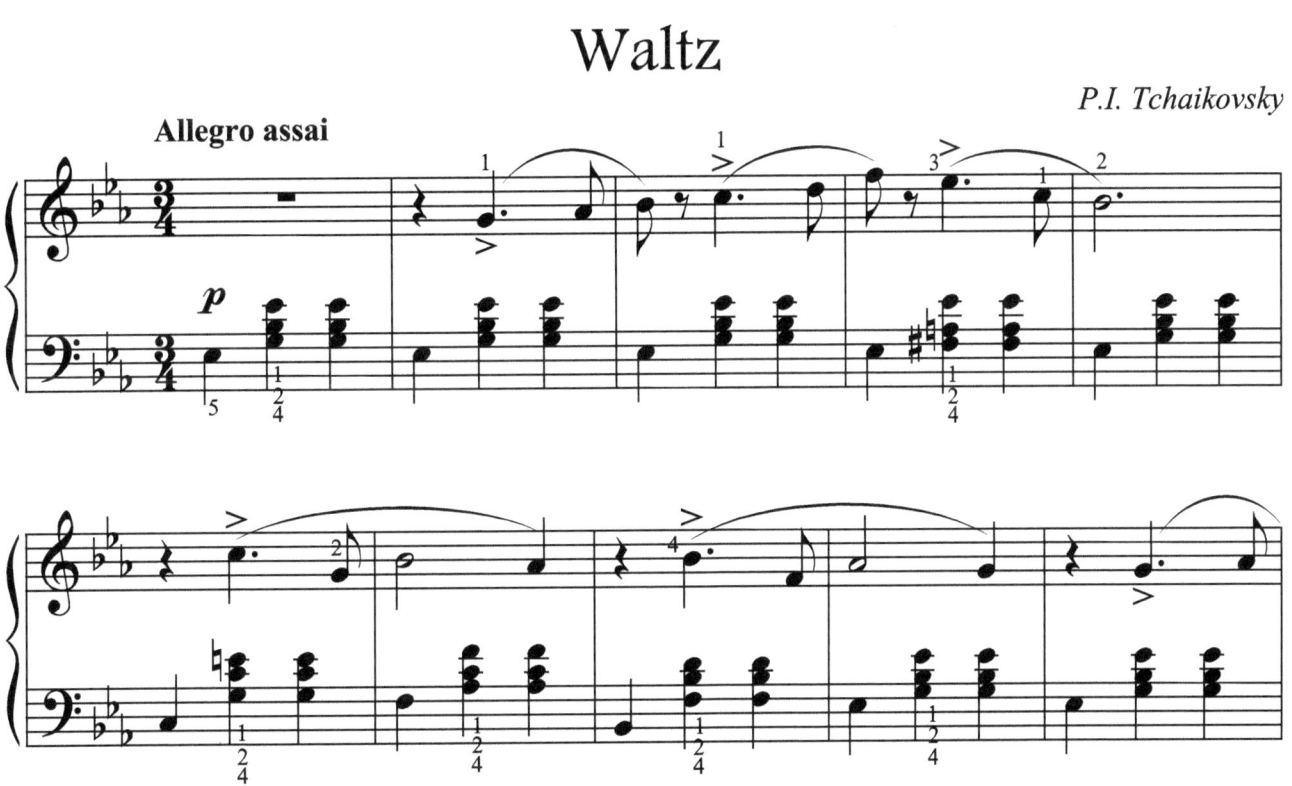

New Doll

Allegro

P.I. Tchaikovsky

Rebecca: I want more dancing!

Teacher: Then we will have two more dances – the *mazurka* and the *polka*. Let's discuss the nature of those dances. Who can tell me where those dances originated?

Jenny: The *mazurka* is Polish and the *polka* is a Czech dance!

Tom: Chopin composed beautiful *mazurkas* for the piano.

Mary: The accent in a *mazurka* falls on the second or third beat.

Rebecca: I know how to dance the *polka*: one two, one two, one two…

Mary: *Polka* is based on gentle half-steps and turning skips!

Teacher: Tchaikovsky grew up in a household where parties featured these popular dances. The dances in his *Album* are reminiscent of his own childhood.

Mazurka

Polka

Moderato
Tempo di Polka

P.I. Tchaikovsky

FOLK TUNES

Teacher: One of the most significant sources of inspiration for any composer is folk music. In Tchaikovsky's *Album*, we can find songs from many different nations: Italy, Germany, France, and, of course, Russia.

The influence of Italian folk songs can be found in *Neapolitan Song,* the theme of which was adapted into Tchaikovsky's *Children's Album* from his ballet *Swan Lake*.

Neapolitan Song

P.I. Tchaikovsky

sempre staccato la mano sinistra

62

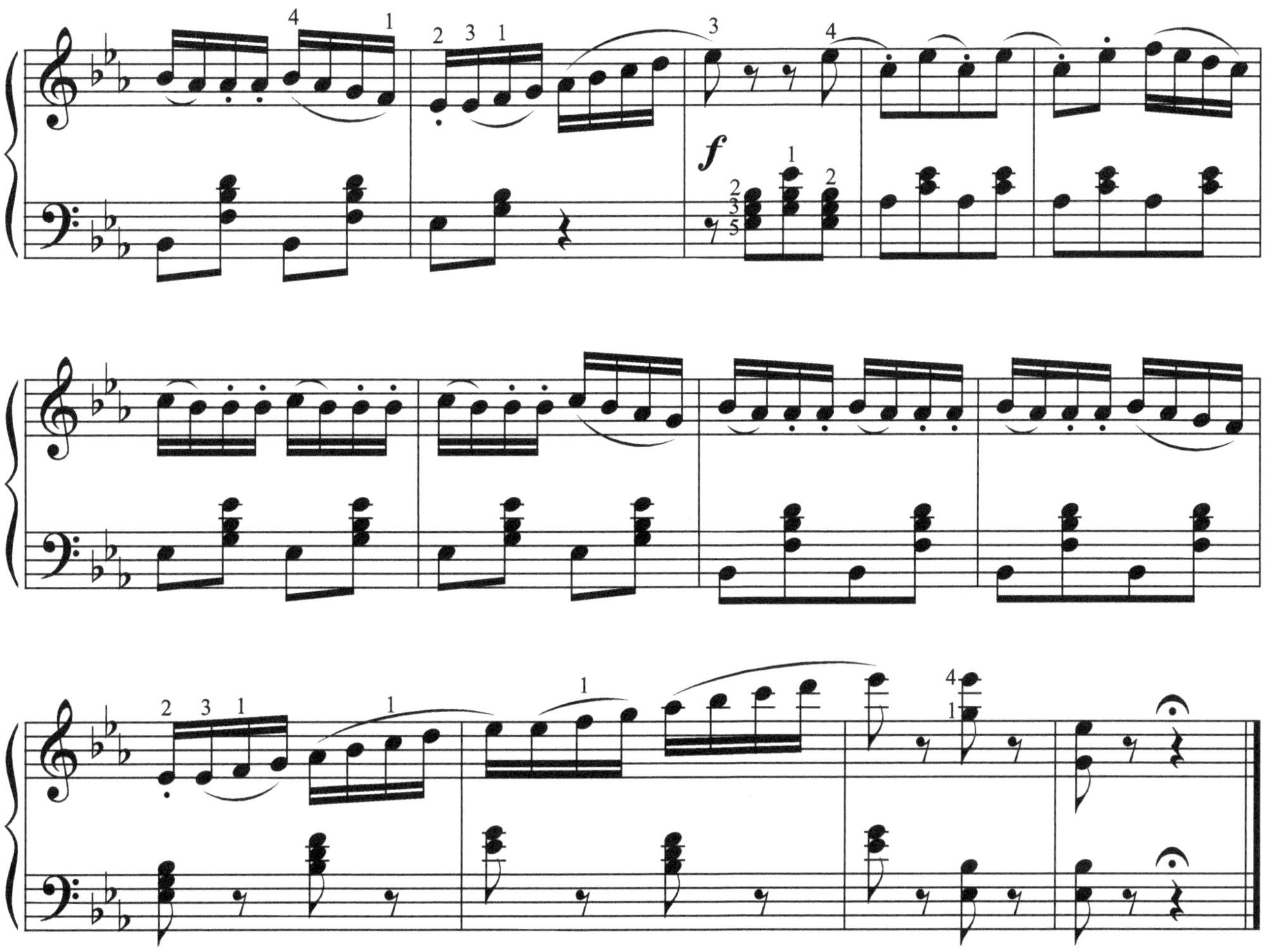

Teacher: An original ancient French folk melody from the 16th century is heard in *Old French Song*. The composer used the same tune in his opera, *Girl from Orleans*, in which the song is performed by choir of minstrels using harps for accompaniment. In the middle section of *Old French Song*, you can imagine the sound of the harp in the staccato accompaniment in the left hand.

Old French Song

P.I. Tchaikovsky

Molto moderato

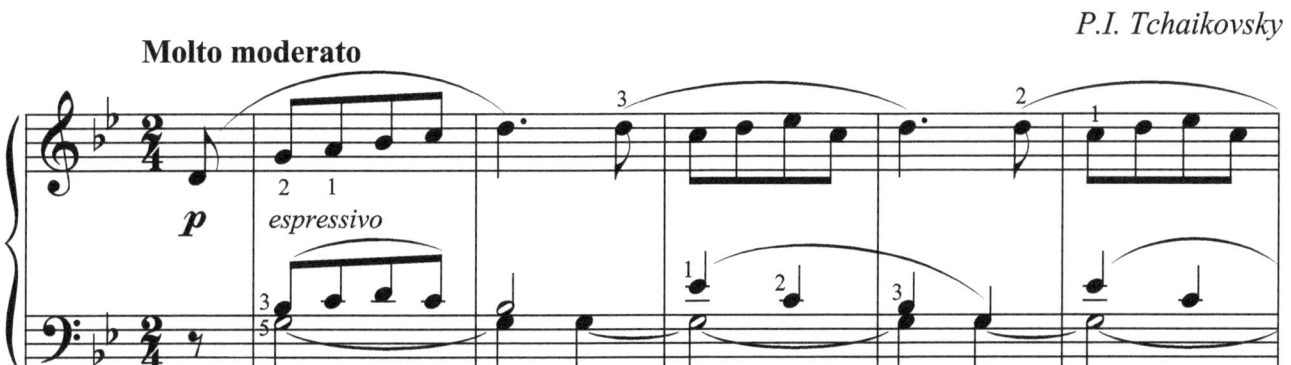

Teacher: A Tyrolean tune was used for *German Song*.

In it, Tchaikovsky imitates Tyrolean yodelling, a type of singing that changes rapidly in pitch from the chest voice to falsetto. As a result, the sound goes, 'high-low-high-low.'

Teacher: *Russian Song* and *Kamarinskaya* are based on Russian folk themes.

In the *Russian Song*, the composer varies an original Russian theme, finishing each cadence in a different mode — alternating major and minor. This is very common in Russian folk songs.

Russian Song

P.I. Tchaikovsky

Teacher: *Kamarinskaya* is an energetic dance, accompanied by different instruments. The staccato melody in the right hand imitates the balalaika, a traditional Russian instrument. A drone bass and the repetitive motives in the left hand remind the sound of the Russian harmonica.

Kamarinskaya

P.I. Tchaikovsky

Teacher: Tchaikovsky composed part of his *Album* in a Ukrainian village where he would often hear the street performers. The sound of the Russian harmonica is heard in his *Harmonica Player*.

Jenny: How do you play the Russian harmonica?

Teacher: The Russian harmonica is a Russian folk instrument resembling a simplified version of an accordion. This is an instrument in the shape of a box that a player holds in his or her hands. The sound is produced by squeezing in and drawing out a bellows (we can clearly hear how Tchaikovsky imitates this action with a repetitive chord motive) and by simultaneously pressing buttons on a keyboard. The Russian harmonica was used only for folk music. Moreover, the music usually originated from the area where the instrument was made. Each one was tuned to play in a particular key. Tchaikovsky wrote this piece in B flat major – the most common key for this instrument. In the following piece, imagine a funny person trying to play the Russian harmonica, repeating the tune over and over. Finally, he gets stuck with the sound of the dominant seventh chord. You can imagine him trying it over and over until he grows tired and walks away.

Harmonica Player

P.I. Tchaikovsky

Teacher: Another interesting instrument is introduced in *Organ Grinder Sings*.

Tom: What kind of instrument does an organ grinder play?

Teacher: Organ grinders play the *barrel organ* – a portable mechanical instrument. It looks like a small pipe organ but is activated by turning a crank. The *Organ Grinder Sings* is divided into two parts. The first part uses the melody of an original Venetian song Tchaikovsky heard from a street singer while travelling in Italy. The second part was composed by Tchaikovsky himself. It starts at the end of the 16th bar. Notice the repetitive motive in the left hand supported by a drone bass. This kind of musical effect imitates the sound of an organ.

Ogran Grinder Sings

P.I. Tchaikovsky

WHEN THE SPRING COMES

Teacher: Schumann's *Album* covers the cycle of a whole year divided into the four seasons. The spring season often inspired composers of the Romantic era. The spirit of love and youth is heard in *May, Sweet May*. Schumann's daughter, Eugenia, struggled to perfect this piece. So, her mother advised her to meticulously implement each articulation sign and each change in the dynamics. Later, Eugenia was very grateful for Clara's thoroughness, because the beauty of this music can be fully enjoyed only when each tiny detail of the score is observed and implemented.

May, Sweet May

R. Schumann

Teacher: We face the same difficulties when performing Schumann's *Folk Song*. The full expressiveness of this music can be reached only by the masterful playing of "every tie, every *portamento*, and every bit of phrasing as it was meant" [Eugenia Schumann]. Another interesting feature of *Folk Song* is the contrasting changes in the mood. This brings to mind Beethoven's *Happy-Sad Bagatelle* WoO64, where episodes alternate in character. The same happens in *Folk Song*, where an episode in a plaintive mood is immediately followed by a happy one.

Teacher: In Tchaikovsky's *Album*, the spring radiates through *Song of the Lark*. The lark – a little, hardly noticeable bird with a very strong, high-pitched voice – inspired many Russian composers. One of the most famous Russian romances by Mikhail Glinka, the father of the Russian nationalistic school of composers, is also called *The Lark*. Glinka had a significant influence on all Russian composers of the 19th century, including Tchaikovsky. However, Tchaikovsky, while using Russian folk motives, never aimed to write purely traditional Russian music. He was also highly inspired by Western European composers.

Now, let's explore the sound of this unique bird. In his piece, Tchaikovsky depicts the main features of the lark's singing, including all kinds of ornamentation.

Song of the Lark

P.I. Tchaikovsky

Tom: I know another *Song of the Lark* from Tchaikovsky's *The Seasons*; I also remember the piece *Snowdrop*, the spring flower that grows under the snow in April!

Teacher: Tchaikovsky was commissioned by the editor of a St. Petersburg music magazine to compose a cycle portraying the atmosphere of each month. Thus, there are twelve pieces in *The Seasons*. *Snowdrop* represents April, while *Song of the Lark* represents March.

AN ITALIAN JOURNEY

Teacher: Tchaikovsky began to work on his *Children's Album* in the spring. He returned from Europe, full of impressions. While touring in Italy, he had heard an amazing performance by a young street singer. The memory of this moment is reflected in *Italian Song*. Tchaikovsky uses the original melody he heard from this boy, indicating that the articulation should be followed carefully. This composition should be performed the way Italian folk singers sang their songs – with high expressivity, sincerity, and technical freedom.

Teacher: Schumann also portrays Italy in a few pieces of his *Album*. The most famous one is *Sicilienne*. This piece can be interpreted as a combination of two folk dances. One is gracious and playful while the other is energetic and joyful.

Jenny: It can also be one dance. In the first part, the girls are dancing, and the second part is for boys.

Teacher: It could be either way! It is interesting to compare the second "dance" from Schumann's *Sicilienne* with an episode from Tchaikovsky's *Neapolitan Song*:

Teacher: Pay attention to indication of the character in Schumann's piece – "Mischievously."

Tom: Why did Schumann choose this word?

Teacher: Schumann was travelling in Italy, enjoying its atmosphere of happiness and beauty. But at that time, it was not uncommon for travellers to fall victim to the craftiness of some Italian traders.

Sicilienne

R. Schumann

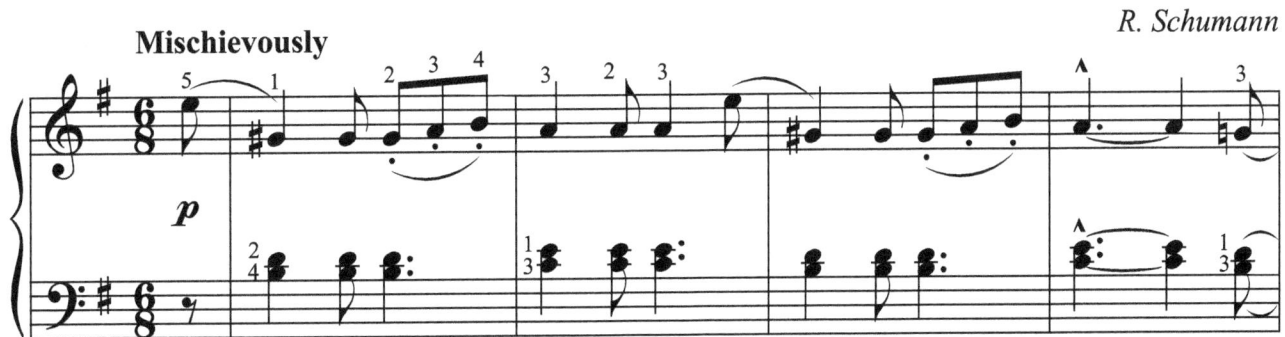

Fine

From the beginning
without repetition
to the word **Fine**

WINTER TIME

Teacher: While Schumann's *Album* spans an entire year, Tchaikovsky's cycle spans just twenty four hours. A child in his *Album* wakes up on a winter morning, looks into the window and sees...

Jenny: What?

Teacher: A typical Russian winter landscape – gloomy and freezing. Full of sadness and anguish, the theme reminds us of a Russian song. Tchaikovsky describes a restless spirit in the ascending and descending sequences of sharp, icy harmonies (accentuated dissonant chords with resolution to the tonic and dominant). He often used sequences for dramatic development.

Mary: It sounds like wind swirling a tail of snowflakes back and forth.

Teacher: Yes, and, thus, the melody line shouldn't be broken up by rests. It has to be performed on a "long breath." The tempo indicated in the music is *fast*, but the performance shouldn't be energetic. Otherwise, the "singing" qualities and tormented character of the music will be shattered.

Winter Morning

P.I. Tchaikovsky

Tom: How did Schumann portray winter in his *Album*?

Teacher: There are two winter scenes in his *Album*: The first piece sounds like a requiem. It resembles a theme from Tchaikovsky's most tragic work, the final part of *Symphony No. 6, The Pathétique*.

Winter Time

R. Schumann

Mary: What happens next with the child from Tchaikovsky's *Album*?

Teacher: Apparently his mother entered the room, for we return to the major key in the piece *Mama*. The melody lines in the soprano and bass are built from short expressive motives. The music sounds bright and gentle; however, from the very beginning, we sense a sign of gradually-developing agitation.

Rebecca: Is the child scared because there is a wolf outside?

Tom: Maybe the child is moody and uncomfortable because of the gloomy weather?

Teacher: Could be! The rhythm and structure of the phrases vary; in addition, the dynamics develop from piano to forte, enhancing the dramatic atmosphere of the first section. In the end of the piece, where the triple pulse is changed to a duple one, the short phrases with accentuated dissonant motives bring back a memory of *Winter Morning*.

Mary: Maybe composer wants to say that the child looked out of the window again...

Mama

P.I. Tchaikovsky

FAIRYTALES

Jenny: How about evenings? Is there a lullaby for a baby or something soothing?

Teacher: In Schumann's *Album*, there is *Humming Song*, which was written when Schumann's eldest son, Ludwig, was born. Notice that in the left hand, the composer recreates the effect of rocking the baby's crib. The simple melody in the right hand is based on a five-note motive. The same compositional techniques were implemented in *Melody* and *Little Song without Words.* I guess Schumann wanted children to exercise a particular piano technique, as well as show them the use of a single theme in composition.

Humming Song

R. Schumann

Melody

R. Schumann

Teacher: In old times in Russia, children often had nannies who told fairytales to children before their bedtime. So in the evening, Tchaikovsky has Nanny tell us a musical story. She tells it in a very intriguing way, pausing after short motives to enhance curiosity. In the middle part of the piece, you'll feel a sort of anticipation.

Tom: As if the children are eager to know the end of the story.

Teacher: Or there is probably something scary, as is often the case in fairytales. The "anticipation" is portrayed by repetitive syncopation in the right hand and a chromatic sequence in the left hand. We already know that Tchaikovsky uses sequences to enhance tension.

Nanny Tells a Story

P.I. Tchaikovsky

Teacher: The fairytale continues and in the next piece we meet nobody else but… Baba Yaga!

Mary: Sounds dangerous! Who's she?

Teacher: She is an old witch from Russian fairytales!

Rebecca: I know, I know! She has a hooked nose and a broom!

Tom: Is she very scary? What does she do? Where does she live?

Teacher: She lives in a house that stands on huge chicken legs. Those crooked legs give the house phenomenal mobility. For example, following Baba Yaga's order, it can turn around quickly, hiding its entrance. Baba Yaga flies over the forest in a huge mortar (a cup-shaped container made of wood), using a broom as a rudder, and she aims to eat children who get lost in the forest. Luckily, she never succeeds. Tchaikovsky introduces Baba Yaga with short repetitive ascending motives, finishing them with a *sforzando* and employing tritones (augmented forth or diminished fifth). The dissonant sound of the tritones heightens the tension.

Rebecca: It sounds like she is jumping from the bushes and saying, "Boo!!!"

Teacher: It does sound pretty humorous. As I mentioned, she is not necessarily an evil witch. In the middle part, Tchaikovsky introduces the *toccata* again.

Tom: It sounds like *The Hobby Horses*, but not as lively.

Teacher: Agreed! We can imagine Baba Yaga riding her mortar, making circles above the forest.

Baba Yaga

P.I. Tchaikovsky

107

Tom: I like scary tales! Is there something scary in Schumann's *Album*?

Teacher: Initially, Schumann deemed his creation a *Christmas Album*. There is a strange man that originated from pagan legends called *Knight Rupert* who, during Christmastime, comes to the houses along with Santa Claus (originally he was called Saint Nicolas) and punishes children for misbehaviour. Schumann's main theme starts in unison, rising from the lower register to the top of the keyboard, invoking a feeling of an unavoidable danger.

Tom: We can imagine that Knight Rupert is climbing the stairs to the living room!

Jenny: What happens to the children?

Teacher: Apparently the children crawled under the table and were sitting there shaking in fear. In the middle part of the composition, you will hear that tremolos form a plaintive melody line.

Jenny: Did Knight Rupert punish them?

Teacher: I believe they were good children because in the same middle part, you'll hear a new, more encouraging theme.

Mary: Is it Santa Claus who is talking to the children?

Teacher: We imagine that Santa doesn't let his partner take any action. Instead, he gives presents to the children and then Santa and Knight Rupert leave the house. Schumann repeats the first theme as if the two walk down the stairs.

Knight Rupert

CHORALES AND CAROLS

Teacher: Starting his cycle from the *Morning Prayer*, Tchaikovsky recreates the feeling of the Divine presence in his last piece, *In the Church*. Again we hear beautiful choral harmonies. In both pieces, the composer uses a similar technique for the final part: The sound of the repetitive bass in the left hand supporting descending chords in the right, imitating the sound of church bells. The bell effect was one of the most popular tools among Russian composers.

In the Church

P.I. Tchaikovsky

Teacher: In Schumann's *Album*, there are two chorales as well. We have already explored the first one, *Chorale*. Do you remember that it was simple and short? Schumann develops it into a more complex polyphonic work. He doubles the top voice and adds an additional ornamental voice. Thus, it is called the *Figured Chorale* – the word Figured is indicative of the ornamentation in the music. In its technique, this version of the chorale resembles the famous *Organ Prelude* in F Minor by J.S. Bach. Bach's prelude was arranged for the piano by Busoni, a 19th century pianist and composer. Like Mendelssohn, Busoni was one of the composers who dedicated part of his professional life to the exposure of Bach's music.

Figured Chorale

R. Schumann

Teacher: The chorale brings us to the last piece of Schumann's cycle – *New Year's Eve*. It is reminiscent of *Remembrance*. Notice that both pieces are composed in A major. It is also worth observing that the structure of the main themes is very similar. Both are shaped with almost the same intervals. However, the themes move in opposite directions. The melody in *Remembrance* starts with sorrowful descending intonations, while in *New Year's Eve* the melody moves up with a questioning tone.

Tom: Is *New Year's Eve* also written in the genre of *Song without Words*?

Teacher: No, because we can't find an accompaniment in the music necessary for the song genre. The piece sounds more like a chorale. It actually reminds me of a Christmas carol. Both compositions reflect the same mix of feelings – nostalgia, warmth, and hope.

Jenny: Why does the New Year's celebration sound sad?

Teacher: Schumann named the first version of this final piece, *At the End*. I suppose that Schumann felt a bit sad when he completed his beautiful *Album*. From another point of view, feelings of nostalgia often come at the end-of-a-year cycle, while warmth and kindness, which penetrate the whole piece, symbolize hope for happiness in the New Year.

New Year's Eve

In moderate tempo

R. Schumann

INDEX OF MUSIC

R. Schumann, Album for the Young, Op. 68 (1848)

No1. Melody 100

No 2. Soldier's March 14

No 3. Humming Song 98

No 4. Chorale 10

No 5. Little Song without Words 22

No 8. Wild Horseman 32

No 9. Folk Song 78

No 10. Happy Farmer 20

No 11. Sicilienne 87

No 12. Knight Rupert 110

No 13. May, Sweet May 74

No 16. First Loss 44

No 19. Romance 26

No 28. Remembrance 24

No 35. Mignon 47

No 38. Winter Time 94

No 42. Figured Chorale 116

No 43. New Year's Eve 119

P. I. Tchaikovsky, Children's Album, Op. 39 (1879)

No 1. Morning Prayer 9

No 2. Winter Morning 91

No 3. Playing Hobby-Horses 34

No 4. Mama 96

No 5. March of the Wooden Soldiers 16

No 6. Sick Doll 39

No 7. Funeral March 41

No 8. Waltz 49

No 9. New Doll 54

No 10. Mazurka 56

No 11. Russian Song 66

No 12. Harmonica Player 70

No 13. Kamarinskaya 67

No 14. Polka 59

No 15. Italian Song 85

No 16. Old French Song 63

No 17. German Song 65

No 18. Neapolitan Song 61

No 19. Nanny Tells a Story 103

No 20. Baba Yaga 107

No 21. Sweet Dream 28

No 22. Song of the Lark 81

No 23. Organ Grinder Sings 73

No 24. In the Church 114

INDEX OF ILLUSTRATIONS

Elsie Lu (7 years old)

Wild Horseman 31

Organ Grinder Sings 72

Song of the Lark 80

Nanny Tells a Story 102

Baba Yaga 106

Esther Lee (15 years old)

Mignon 46

Italian Song 84

Jingchen Ma (8 years old)

Happy Farmer 19

First Loss 43

Rebecca Bukhman (4 years old)

New Doll 53

Sarah Yang (7 years old)

Soldier's March 13

Rada Bukhman

Sick Doll 38

Funeral March 40

Harmonica Player 69

Winter Morning 90

In the Church 113

New Year's Eve 118

www.ingramcontent.com/pod-product-compliance
Lightning Source LLC
Chambersburg PA
CBHW041153230426
43673CB00036B/506